THE

ANGLO-SAXON RACE:

ITS

History, Character, and Destiny.

AN ADDRESS

BEFORE

THE SYRACUSE UNIVERSITY,

At Commencement, June 21, 1875.

BY

DEXTER A. HAWKINS, A.M.,

OF THE NEW YORK BAR.

PRINTED BY NELSON & PHILLIPS,

805 BROADWAY, NEW YORK.

1875.

With Compliments of

DEXTER A. HAWKINS.

"Jam redit et virgo, redeunt Saturnia regna.
Jam nova progenies coelo dimittitur alto."

ADDRESS.

MR. CHANCELLOR, AND LADIES AND GENTLEMEN:

When invited to appear before you this year by the eminent scholar and Christian gentleman who presides over this University, the striking growth of the Institution, and the energy, liberality and enthusiasm of the people in endowing and supporting it, suggested to me as a theme,—

THE ANGLO-SAXON RACE:

ITS HISTORY, CHARACTER, AND DESTINY.

An eminent English writer of the last century described a branch of this race (the American) as "A great people formed into free communities, under governments which have no religious tests and establishments."

In every period of history some single race or nation acts the leading part. The others, like the minor characters in a tragedy, circle around it, content to contribute to its success and share in its glory. Political power and the arts of civilization are for the time being intrusted to this one; and while playing its destined *role* in the great epic poem of human life, its sister races struggle in vain to surpass it, or yield to the decrees of Providence and acknowledge its superiority.

Persia, Egypt, Greece and Rome, were each for centuries star actors of the highest excellence. They combined intellectual skill and physical force. The magnificent ruins in Asia; the pyramids, temples and monuments of Egypt; the literature, laws and works of art of Greece and Rome, attest this. But Cyrus, Darius and Xerxes, Rameses and the Ptolemies; the cultured worshipers at the shrine of Apollo and Minerva; Solon, Pericles, Socrates and Plato; the twelve Cesars, rulers of the world; and the political and social systems which each represented, have passed off the stage.

Another and a different race is now before us, one that is and ever has been distinguished for its energy, activity, love of individual liberty and of national independence. From its composite ancestry and character, it is now called the Anglo-Saxon. Our own country is, perhaps, its most promising and vigorous representative. The poet Cowley said to our fathers:—

> " . . . Your rising glory you shall view,
> Wit, learning, virtue, discipline of war
> Shall for protection to your world repair,
> And fix a long illustrious empire there!"

In sketching the history of a people whose infancy runs back two or three thousand years, authentic records are wanting; but the affinity of languages often enables the student to discover and bring to light the important, yet otherwise hidden, facts of a nation's early life. The great antiquity of the Saxons compels us to resort to this source of information.

The various languages of Europe naturally range themselves into three distinct families or classes, the Celtic, the Gothic, and the Sclavonic; each having characteristics peculiar to itself, yet showing a latent bond of union which indicates that they and the races speaking them had somewhere in the distant past a common origin. The cultivated nations of modern Europe and of America are all of Aryan stock, or, as some writers call them, Japhetians, from Japhet, son of Noah; but 4,000 years have made wide distinctions in language, character, and name between the different branches of this great mother race. Sanskrit is, perhaps, the nearest to the Aryan, of any language now known; and philological investigation traces back to that source roots of all modern cultivated tongues, and indicates that their origin is not only Asiatic, but Aryan. This view is confirmed by the few passages of ancient history extant upon this point. All the witnesses we can summon from languages, from history, and from monumental stones, tell us that Europe was peopled by three great streams of population from Asia, which have come to be designated as the Celtic, the Gothic, and Sclavonic streams or races.

The first of these three races was the Celtic, or Keltic. The origin of this name is doubtful. Some look upon the stem "Cel," or "Kel," as a simple primitive word formed by a guttural and a lingual; some derive it from the Gaelic "ceilt," an inhabitant of the forest; others from the Welsh "celt," a covert, or "celtiad," one who dwells in a covert, or from "celu," to hide; while others say that it is from the Latin "celare," to conceal, and was given to them by the Romans because they concealed their habitations in the depths of the forests and in caves. Another writer illustrates the name by three Greek words meaning to conceal something from some one, and infers from this the antiquity of the happy, and often entertaining, faculty of narrating fictions, that some perverse minds have thought characterized the true Celt. Another authority says, that this habit results simply from a desire to please; and hence, unlike a certain ancient Greek, the Celt is said to be given to saying things agreeable rather than things disagreeable though true. This race was afterward closely pressed upon by their more powerful, warlike, and ambitious Gothic successors, and they gradually retired and dwindled away upon the western shores of Europe and the British Islands, till few are left except the inhabitants of the coast of France, the extreme northern Scotch or Highlanders, the Welsh, and the Irish. Their emigration from Asia is earlier than the historic period. It occurred before the invention of letters, when nations had no means, save vague tradition, of treasuring up their story and handing it down to posterity. The arts and sciences among them were as yet hardly born; hence their exit from Asia or entrance into Europe was marked by no monuments that might, like those of Egypt, through their astronomical inscriptions, tell to the men of science, three thousand years afterward, the date of their erection.

Races of men have great functions to perform in the drama of human life upon this globe; and when performed, they and their works, in the course of Providence, imperceptibly melt away. Their stronger and better elements are absorbed by their more vigorous and manly, I might say godly, successors; while the weaker ones, being of no further use to humanity, sink away, and disappear in the sea of oblivion. The Celts, as a distinctive branch of the human family, long since reached their climax, and are now too small in number to become again noted. As an element, a factor, in the composition of races, they are of great value; but as a separate and independent result they have ceased to exist.

The Gothic or Scythian immigrations came next. These were a bold, roving, nomadic people, who spread themselves over the mountains, and into the vast forests, plains, and marshes of Europe, till they occupied nearly the whole continent. This second stream is peculiarly interesting to us, because from its branches have sprung the Anglo-Saxons, the Lowland Scotch, the Danes, Norwegians, Germans, Lombards, Normans, and Franks; not only our immediate ancestors, but also those of the most celebrated nations of modern Europe. They made their appearance in Europe, according to Homer, Herodotus, Strabo, Pliny, Ptolemaius of Alexandria, about seven or eight hundred years before the Christian era.

The third and last great influx was the Sclavonic. This has occupied Russia, Poland, Eastern Prussia, Moravia, and Bohemia; a race once possessed of great power and glory, for their very name is derived from the word "Sclava," which in the original tongue meant "fame," "glory," or "renown." If the Pan-Slavic dreams of the Muscovite statesmen, to unite this whole race under one head and to develop and perfect it by a rigorous system of universal education, is ever realized, the Sclavs will have at some future period a great *rôle* to play.

But the next act in the world's drama is cast for another people, and it does not require a prophet's eye to discern that, for centuries to come, the Gothic nations are to lead the world in social, political, material and intellectual progress. Of these the Anglo-Saxons, from the circumstances of their history and their enterprising character, are admirably qualified for the noblest destiny. Their history naturally divides itself into four periods.

The *first* extends from their origin in Asia, about the year 1000 B. C., or the date of the Temple of Solomon, to the establishment of their power in England, A. D. 500.

The *second*, from that time to the Norman conquest, A. D. 1066.

The *third*, from this epoch to the English revolution and the settlement of America, A. D. 1650.

The *fourth*, from those two events to the present time.

About 1,000 years before Christ a martial people of Aryan stock ruled the part of Asia about the Caspian Sea, and were generally designated in history as Scythians. They carried on wars against the Assyrians and the Medes. Some national difficulty, threatening if not producing civil war, arose among them about 800 B.C., and the younger branch, called the Sakai, moved west into Asia Minor, and into the part of Europe east and north of the Black Sea. They attacked the Persians, who then ruled Asia Minor, defeated Cyrus the emperor, captured the most fertile province of Armenia, named it after themselves, Sakasina, or the land of the Sakai, and made themselves entirely at home there. They became so celebrated that the Persians finally gave their name to all the Scythians, of whom, as we have stated, they were only a branch.

Strabo and Pliny, at the beginning of the Christian era, speak of them as Sakai Suna, or sons of Sakai, and the most distinguished of the people of Scythia; and of this province as having from them taken the name of Sakasina. This important fact gives a locality to our early ancestors, and accounts for the Persian words, several hundred in number, that occur in the Anglo-Saxon language. One writer says that Sakai-Suna became for ease of utterance contracted into Saksuna, and then into Saxon; but this etymology of Saxon may be akin to the derivation given in the "Diversions of Purley" of "King Pepin," from the Greek pronoun "ὅσπερ."

On entering Europe they, in the seventh century before Christ, attacked the Celts or Cimmerians the then occupants of the country about the river Don, drove one part of them back into Asia, and the others west into the center of Europe, and took possession of their lands. The particular rank that they held among the Scythian tribes in their conquering progress across Europe is now unknown; but we may justly infer that it was not unworthy their previous and their after history. We find them at the beginning of the Christian era inhabiting a small territory at the mouth of the river Elbe, composed chiefly of three provinces and three small islands;

and from dire necessity just beginning to learn the art of navigation, and to take to the sea for a livelihood. Within these narrow limits was contained a people whose descendants are now leading the world in commercial enterprise and political and religious liberty.

Such is the course of Providence, that empires the most extended and formidable vanish like the morning mist; while tribes scarcely visible, like the springs of a mighty river, glide on to greatness. The largest of these islands was only twenty miles in length; and the most important one, and which contained the greater part of their wealth and a fine harbor, was still smaller. They called it Helgoland, or the sacred island; for, having but one approach by sea, it afforded a safe retreat from their enemies, and was the favorite home of their gods. These, like Mars and Mercury, were the personification of man's baser passions, and presided over war and plundering. No music was more grateful to them than the groans of slaughtered enemies; no offerings more acceptable than the trophies of the battle-field. In accordance with the spirit of that age, the glory of arms alone was sought by those who aspired to the favor of the gods or the honor of men. They, therefore, carried on a continual warfare with the neighboring tribes, but gained little, either in territory or wealth, till the Roman emperors conceived the idea of subjugating all the northern nations of Europe. This was a happy event for the Saxons, and, with a worldly wisdom peculiar to their race, they turned it to their advantage, and began at once to rise in the scale of power and influence.

The Germanic tribes, whose territory lay between them and Rome, being attacked by the more powerful and sanguinary legions of Italy, ceased to oppose them. Their isolated situation secured them from danger, and they were quiet spectators of the fearful struggle about them; or else, at a favorable opportunity, fell upon a weakened neighbor, struck a decisive blow, and annexed his lands and people to their own. This policy, however repugnant to the feelings of a Christian age, pervaded Europe at that time, and was especially practiced by the imperial tyrants of the city of Romulus, whose cruelty, inhumanity, and selfishness give a color of truth to their tradition that their founder had a she-wolf nurse. A surname from a country subdued was a charm that made its generals deaf to the calls of humanity; and with an ignorant and degenerate populace, it was the surest passport to unlimited power.

By the middle of the third century the successes of the Romans were so rapid and great that they threatened the total subversion of the liberties of Germany. To prevent this these wild inhabitants of the woods formed, in the year 240, on the banks of the Rhine, that celebrated confederation, offensive and defensive, in which the peculiar denominations of each tribe were merged in the general name of Franks; which word, as well as the people it designates, has undergone changes until we now call it French. This confederation was a second fortunate event for the Saxons.

The power of Rome now began to crumble. At home, civil wars were consuming the strength of the empire; abroad, its German enemies not only had many losses of property, life, and liberty to avenge, but they had learned the dangerous secret so well illustrated in the late German war, that union is strength; while the Romans, like the French in the same war, seemed bent upon demonstrating the opposite theorem, that discord is weakness. Ambitious of power and wealth, Rome had annexed, by mere brute force, without assimilating its elements, so large a part of Europe, Asia, and Africa, that she was ready almost of her own weight to tumble to pieces.

History teaches that no nation, spread over a wide territory and composed of heterogeneous and discordant elements, can long preserve its integrity. Homogeneity and harmony are essential to permanent national existence.

The advantages of the Frankish league generated others of like character, until the Roman Empire was overwhelmed by this accumulating torrent of enemies, and her western provinces were captured and parceled out among her rude spoilers, whose improved posterity now governs two continents. The Franks, from their locality, were placed in this long contest like a shield between the Saxons and Romans, and were compelled to employ all their resources against the imperial legions. This left the Saxons at liberty to take whatever course promised to contribute most to their own aggrandizement.

A providential event, not originating from themselves, but from a Roman emperor who intended no such results, occurred at the close of the third century, which by directing the attention of the Saxons to maritime exploits on a larger scale, with grander prospects, and to more distant countries than before, exerted an important influence upon their own destiny and that of Europe, and finally of America.

The emperor Probus, harassed by the annual incursions of the barbarous hordes around the Euxine, now the Black Sea, transplanted a large body of various tribes, including Saxons, from the vicinity of the Elbe to that region to serve as a protection against future inroads. But the attachment of mankind to the scenes of their childhood, and their ardent longing when in foreign lands for the country their relatives inhabit, where their most pleasing associations have been formed, where their individual characters have been acquired, and customs like their own exist, are feelings so natural to every bosom, and so common to every age, that it is not surprising that these exiles longed to return to their native wilds. Impelled by this desire, they seized the earliest opportunity of abandoning their foreign settlements and possessing themselves of the ships lying in the adjacent harbors; they formed the daring plan of sailing back to the Rhine, though they were more than two thousand miles distant by sea, with no chart, compass, or pilots, and ignorant of the many islands and shoals and currents of the Black and Mediterranean Seas. Compelled to land wherever they could for supplies, safety, and information, they ravaged the coasts of Asia and Greece. Arriving at Sicily, they attacked and plundered its capital with great slaughter. Beaten about by the winds, often ignorant where they were, seeking subsistence, pillaging to obtain it, and excited to new plunder by the successful depredations they had already committed, they carried their hostility to several districts of Africa. They were driven off that continent by a force sent for the purpose from Carthage. Turning toward Europe, they passed the pillars of Hercules, sailed out into the Atlantic Ocean, rounded the Iberian peninsula, crossed the stormy Bay of Biscay, passed through the British Channel, and finally terminated their remarkable voyage by reaching their fatherland at the mouth of the Elbe.

This wonderful expedition discovered to these adventurers and to their neighbors, to all, in short, who heard and had the courage to imitate, that from the Roman colonies a rich harvest of spoil might be gathered if sought for by sea. It removed the vail of terror that hung over distant oceans and foreign expeditions; for these exiles had desolated every province almost with impunity. They had plunder to exhibit sufficient to fire the avarice of every spectator. They had acquired skill which those who joined them might soon inherit. On land the Roman tactics and discipline were generally invincible, but at sea they were comparatively unskilled and weak. The Saxons perceived this, and immediately turned their whole attention to naval warfare. Like their American descendants, they were cunning and apt at whatever they undertook. Their navy became so effective in a few years that every country of Europe bordering on the sea had contributed to their wealth, and they annoyed the Roman commerce to such a degree that large fleets were fitted out against them, and an officer appointed by the Romans as early as the beginning of the fifth century styled "The Superintendent of the Saxon Shore." These exploits had filled their island with wealth.

At this early period, fourteen hundred years ago, we see beginning to manifest itself that commercial spirit which has always been a great element in Saxon prosperity both national and individual. Their situation on the coast of Europe, near to fertile Roman provinces, yet remote enough to elude vengeful pursuit, and the possession of an island with a harbor so ample and yet so guarded as Helgoland, were in that age strong inducements to piracy. Their occasional service with the Romans or Franks —for they cared but little for whom they fought provided they acquired glory and booty—was admirably calculated to prepare them for such a life. It may be a little mortifying to our national pride to trace our paternity to a nation of freebooters, but it is always safe to admit and stand by the truth; and besides, we can comfort our wounded self-esteem with the recollection that the Roman Republic, once so respected that to be even a "Roman citizen" was a notable honor, sprung from a den of thieves, whose character was so bad that their only way to get wives was to steal them.

The poverty and hardihood of the neighboring tribes poorly repaid the Saxons for expeditions by land, while their sea-girt home and skill on the water was ever inviting them to ravage the ocean. Their approach and retreat were so sudden and unexpected that they met with little opposition, and in their light and swift-sailing barks they easily escaped the clumsy Roman vessels, or else bought immunity from the unprincipled commanders of Rome by permitting them to share a part of their plunder. The Roman government at last discovered the maladministration of their admirals, and ordered the chief officer to be punished. But, trusting to his popularity and strength, he with his legions and ships joined the Saxons, and taught them all that the most celebrated nation then knew of the naval and military art. He was proclaimed Emperor of Rome, and paid the Saxons for their assistance by giving them permission to plunder with impunity every province that did not acknowledge his power. Sixty years afterward they aided another military aspirant for the "Roman Crown" to gain his object by a similar alliance.

Circumstances like these educated the Saxons for the empire of the ocean, and molded them, as by the plastic hand of Providence, to become a race that should excel not only in war, but in commerce, arts, knowledge, and fame, every other people. During the fourth century most of the nations north of the Rhine assumed their name and fought under their flag. They seduced or conquered many allies of the Franks, and at the fall of Rome were masters of the seas, and quite able to compete with any nation of Europe on the land. This ends the first period of their history. In a space of about fourteen hundred years, ending with the fifth century, we have seen them spring up from the valley of the Caspian Sea, conquer and give their name to a part of Asia Minor, move into Europe, pass fifteen hundred miles across it, become a great power on both land and sea, and give their name to the country on the Elbe, a part of which is still called the kingdom of Saxony.

We now come to the second period, namely, the establishment of their power in England, and its continuance down to the Norman conquest. Their ambition was now about to appear in a new field. They had often visited Britain in predatory excursions, and were known as a fearless race of warriors, ready to lend their swords to any enterprise that promised a rich reward. Therefore, when the Britons, abandoned by the Roman legions, found themselves a prey to the fierce and tenacious Scots and Picts, they invited two Saxon princes, the reputed descendants of the god Woden, to come to their assistance. The invitation was readily accepted. Their fleets brought an army across the North Sea, and they soon conquered the enemies of their new allies. But then, instead of going back to the Elbe, they thought the country a sort of new land of Canaan, flowing with milk and honey, and, as usual, made themselves at home in it, sent word to Saxony of the riches and fertility of Britain, and forming an alliance with the warlike Scots and Picts, whom they came to resist, they proceeded to reduce to subjection the Britons, whom they had engaged to protect. Reinforced by two neighboring tribes, called the Angles and Jutes, people of similar manners, customs, and origin to their own, they subdued Britain after a struggle of one hundred and fifty years, divided it into eight kingdoms, and took the name of Anglo-Saxons. Two of these kingdoms, Berenicia and Deira, were afterward united in one, making seven, or the Saxon Heptarchy.

England seems to have been populated at first by the Celts, then visited apparently by the Phœnicians and Carthagenians, and afterward occupied for nearly four centuries by the Romans. It had derived from these successive inhabitants all the benefits that each could impart. But now it was possessed by a new kind of people, who had been gradually formed, amid the wars and vicissitudes of the Germanic continent, to manners, laws, and customs peculiarly their own, and adapted, as the great result has shown, to produce national and social institutions superior to those of either Asia, Africa, Greece, or Rome. Our Saxon ancestors brought with them for those times an elevated domestic and moral character, and the rudiments of new political, juridical, and intellectual blessings. They laid the foundations of that national constitution, of that internal polity, of those peculiar customs, and of that vigor and directness of thought, to which the English-speaking races are indebted for the high social and political rank which they now hold.

But as the Saxon power increased in Britain it declined on the continent. Charlemagne, at the close of the eighth century, became emperor of the Franks. He was to their armies what Alexander the Great was to the Macedonians, and Cæsar to the Romans, and Bonaparte to the French. He organized and led their forces against the Saxons; and after one of the most obstinate and bloody wars that history records, they were conquered in seven pitched battles, and lost their predominance on the continent, and have ever since acted a secondary, but not obscure, part among the Gothic States of Europe.

Saxony is still a kingdom, though stripped of its ancient honors, and presents a people highly intellectual and cultivated. Its nobles have been emperors of Germany, and from them have sprung some of the most illustrious princes of middle Europe, princes who, by their activity, leagues, conquests, and love of independence, have done much for German civilization. Saxony has the honor of having given birth to Luther, the great reformer of Christianity; and its chieftains of having supported and enabled him to carry through his emancipation of mind from the shackles of papacy. The rise of the Saxon nation on the continent has therefore been singularly propitious for human improvement.

The Saxons were, indeed, in their early days, without the knowledge and culture of letters possessed by the effeminate and enslaved inhabitants of Greece and Italy; but there is an education of mind, distinct from the literary, which is gradually imparted by the contingencies of active life. In this, which is always the education of the largest portion of mankind, our Saxon ancestors were never deficient. They had been nurtured in the rugged school of adversity, and amid the wilds of Asia and Europe, or compassed by the stormy ocean, they had learned to meet unmoved the most appalling dangers, and had carved out for themselves a lofty name. On the transfer of their power to the Island of Britain they would, in the midst of ease and luxury, have lost fortitude of character had not the ambitious rulers of the Heptarchy, each striving to extend the limits of his own kingdom at the expense of his neighbor's, kept it constantly exercised. Thus, their separation into several independent States, though not conducive to refinement of manners and mental improvement, preserved and developed to a surprising degree the practical and active talents of the Saxons. But as the number of kings were diminished by the fortunes of war or the accidents of life, the people underwent a corresponding change. Peace and plenty brought degeneracy and inefficiency.

A nation that both believes and practices Christianity as taught by our Saviour can endure prosperity; but without some such active, controlling, and elevating sentiment in the mass of the people, nothing but the rude trials, schooling, and spurs of adversity can help men and nations steadily on in the course of improvement. The majority of the Saxons were at this period worshipers of Woden and Thor; and the few that bore the name of Christians were scarcely worthy to be called disciples of Gregory, to whose benevolence they owed their conversion. He was passing through the slave-market of Rome one day, when the white skins, flowing locks, and beautiful countenances of some British youths standing there for sale drew his attention. Being informed that the dwellers in Britain were all of that fair complexion, and pagans, too, his heart was moved, and he exclaimed with a sigh, "What a pity that such a beauteous frontispiece should cover a mind so void of internal graces!" When he heard them called Angles, "It suits them," he said; "they have angel faces, and ought to be coheirs of angels in heaven." The name of their province, Deira, was so like the Latin words *De ira* ("from wrath") that it seemed to his simple mind to imply that they ought to be snatched from the wrath of God. The harmony of their king's name, Ella, with the idea then floating in his mind, completed the impression of the whole scene, and there burst forth from his pious lips the exclamation, "Halleluiah! the praise of the creative Deity must be sung in these regions." When Gregory became pope, one of his first acts was to send a body of missionaries to the Saxon princes. But the religion they taught, besides being corrupted almost to idolatry by the forms and image worship of the Church of Rome, was received by many of the heathen sages on the express condition that it should afford them greater worldly riches and honor than the worship of their gods of stone; hence its effect for a long time was little, if any, better than the paganism it supplanted. But God had a work for them to do, and he found them out in their degeneracy, and administered to them a tonic the benefit of which is felt even to this day.

The vikings, or sea-kings, sometimes in English history called the Danes, of the same race as the Saxons, and preserving the manly virtues of the days of Hengist and Horsa, swarmed the ocean from the countries about the Baltic, and invaded Britain. These restless monarchs were a scourge to Europe for a century, and were universally detested for their cruelties. But their innate energy of character contributed an important element to Saxon greatness.

Nations, like individuals, unless they are compelled to struggle in the battle of life, or are ruled by a high sense of duty, will fall into a moral and physical decline. The history of most tropical countries so clearly demonstrates this, that we justly assume it is a blessing rather than a curse, that man, by the sweat of his brow, is compelled to earn his daily bread ; for where the fruits of the earth sufficient for his sustenance grow spontaneously, his mental and moral condition approaches that of brutes. The Saxons were on the verge of a moral and national decline, when the invasion of the sea-kings, like a scourge sent from God to chasten them for being untrue to themselves, awakened their energies, and impressed upon them the undying love of liberty and the freedom of the seas, characteristic of that lawless race.

Perhaps we can form a clearer idea of the influence of the sea-kings upon the Saxons by a glance at some of their customs. In the families of their princes, one of the male children only remained at home and inherited the government; the rest were exiled to the ocean, to wield their scepters amid the turbulent waters, or lose them. All men of royal descent who assumed piracy as a profession enjoyed the title of king, though without any kingdom or visible nation, with no wealth but their ships, no force but their crews, and no hope but in their swords. Never to sleep under a smoky roof, nor to indulge in the cheerful cup around the social hearth, were the boasts of these watery sovereigns. While the eldest son ascended the paternal throne, the others, furnished with vessels fully equipped as their only patrimony, hastened, like petty Neptunes, to establish their kingdoms on the water. When death overtook them, the royal tomb of the viking was his ship. His lifeless form was laid out in state upon the quarter-deck, and his vessel with his body and arms was drawn ashore and buried. Some of these tombs on the coast of Norway have lately, after a thousand years of burial, been discovered.

So honorable and lucrative was their profession at one period, that private individuals who possessed the means were eager to enter it. Parents were so anxious to have their children engage in this dangerous and malevolent occupation, that, at their death, they would order all their wealth to be destroyed, except enough to enable their offspring once to hoist their sails on the deep in a well-equipped vessel. Inherited property was despised. That affluence alone was esteemed which danger had endeared. No one was held truly noble, no one respected, who did not ravage the ocean in summer, and in winter return to his home with ships laden with booty.

Trained in such a school, the sea-kings exhibited the ruder, sterner virtues in the highest perfection. To a stubborn courage and unyielding will, they added a nobleness of bearing and suavity of manners that gained them friends among their enemies, and preserved their authority in England, though few in numbers, for a century and a half. The most powerful sovereign of this line, Canute the Great, was even a patron of learning and religion; and, unlike most men, the more he enjoyed the favors of fortune, the greater was his morality and meekness of heart. He thought it not beneath the dignity of the ruler of six kingdoms to descend from his throne and teach his subjects lessons of humility. Under the labors and influence of such sovereigns as Canute, and of Alfred the Great, the most distinguished king of the Saxon line, and one of the most remarkable men the world has produced, ignorance and idolatry began to vanish from the island, and give place to intelligence and Christianity. Churches had been built, colleges founded, and teachers appointed for both. The nation began to feel the movings of a spirit that required a wider field for action than the circle of this island, and the example and leadership of a king and nobility more imbued with the spirit of the rising Christian civilization than the Saxons.

Britain was called by the Latin poets "a country wholly cut off from the rest of the world." But it was ordained by the great Ruler, without whose knowledge neither a sparrow falls to the ground, nor a change comes over a nation, that both for its own benefit and that of mankind it should for the future become intimately connected with the affairs of the world. Edward the Confessor having no issue, and influenced both by friendship for William, Duke of Normandy, and by admiration of his noble qualities, desired the British crown to fall to him. That powerful duke, while on a visit to Edward, had seen the wealth and fertility of the Saxon kingdom, and was nothing loth. When Edward died, William invaded England with a fleet of three thousand vessels, carrying sixty thousand men well equipped, and officered by the most illustrious nobles of Normandy, Flanders, Brittany, and France. At the battle of Hastings he conquered and killed Harold, the Saxon king, and mounted the throne of England.

This was another fortunate event for the development of the Anglo-Saxons, otherwise the physical in their civilization would have overborne the intellectual and esthetic; and they would have been of a nature though strong, yet too coarse and uncultivated, for the highest eminence in an enlightened period. As in architecture, the Doric column, though remarkable for simplicity and strength, is by no means so much admired in a polished age as the more beautiful Corinthian, with its fluted shaft and capital adorned with acanthus leaves. The polite luxury of the Norman, though of the same Gothic race, presented a striking contrast to the less refined tastes of the Saxon. He loved to display his magnificence, not in huge piles of food and hogsheads of strong drink, but in large and stately palaces, rich armor, gallant horses, well-ordered tournaments; banquets, delicate and toothsome, rather than abundant; and wines excellent rather for their exquisite flavor than for their intoxicating power. That chivalrous spirit which exercised so powerful an influence on the politics, morals, and manners of all the European nations, was found in the highest exaltation among the Norman nobles. Those nobles were distinguished for their graceful bearing and insinuating address, for their skill in negotiation, and for a natural eloquence. It was the boast of one of their historians that the

Norman gentlemen were orators from the cradle. Saxon civilization without the Norman element might be compared to a huge Gothic structure of unhewn granite: with it, those majestic but naked halls, though still Gothic, are filled with all the refinements of art, and the comforts of social life. By means of the continental possessions which William brought to the British Crown, and through the system of diplomacy which afterward, in the fifteenth century, sprang up, a door was opened for Anglo-Saxon enterprise to wield great influence in the national affairs of Europe. Their power came to be felt at every court on the continent. Their armies gathered laurels in every country, and their fleets on every sea; while they themselves, protected by their wooden walls, as their navy is called, have almost forgotten that Albion's soil has been thrice possessed by victorious invaders: Romans, Saxons, Normans.

At this point let us take a hasty survey of the civil polity of the Saxons at the time of the Norman conquest. Society was divided into four distinct grades:—

First. The king, who till a late period was elective, though birth and the wishes of the deceased sovereign were generally followed.

Second. The nobles, or thanes. These were of two classes: the king's thanes, who held land of him and attended him at court, and the ordinary thanes, or manorial lords. Any man could be admitted to this second class of thanes who had made three long sea voyages in his own ship, or who owned five hundred acres of land and had a chapel, a kitchen, a hall, and a bell; though these factitious thanes were by no means so much respected as those of generous blood. The term thane after the conquest was discarded for that of baron.

Third. The freemen. These were of two classes, the socmen, or those who had a permanent lease of the land on which they lived, and the ceorles, or tenants-at-will.

Fourth. The slaves, which were by far the most numerous grade, and were also of two kinds: the household slaves and the farm slaves.

The Saxons were always ruled by a king, though he had but little power beyond the will of the thanes. There was this radical difference between the governments of Greece and Rome and those of the Gothic tribes. In the former the State was every thing, the individual nothing: the State was thought to have a perfect right to the property, liberty, and even life, of its citizens. In the latter the individual was every thing and the State comparatively nothing: all rights were thought to exist, to inhere by nature in the individual; and the State could demand nothing from him for public use without giving him an equivalent. Here we find the fundamental principle of civil liberty; that principle which has been so carefully guarded in the English and in all the Anglo-American constitutions, and which was so happily and tersely expressed by Jefferson in the Declaration of Independence. Our rude Saxon ancestors, though under a kingly government, had more real liberty, and a more just appreciation of the true dignity of man, than had the polished citizens of the republics of the Mediterranean. The legislative authority was vested in the witenagemote, or assembly of wise men, which was composed of three classes: the prelates, the aldermen, and the wites, or men of wisdom. The aldermen held office during life, and were chosen not on account of rotundity of person, or natural tendency to steal, but, as the etymology of their name indicates, for their age and experience in affairs. To obtain a seat in the witenagemote, unless by reason of nobility, a man was required to possess forty hides of land, or about five thousand acres. The members were by law secure in their persons, in going to and returning from Parliament, "except they were notorious thieves and robbers." At their elections suffrage was obligatory and compulsory, and failure to attend and vote was punished as a neglect of public duty.

For the administration of justice, and the preservation of good order, the community was divided into counties, hundreds, and tithings. The latter consisted of ten householders, and the presiding officer was called a tithing-man. Each member of the tithing was, in a certain degree, responsible for the behavior of the other nine members. Crimes committed within the precincts of a tithing were charged against it, unless the members of the tithing discovered the offender, or could get twelve men, three from their own number, and three from each of three adjacent tithings, to declare upon their oaths that they believed the tithing innocent. This seems to be the origin in English history of trial by a jury of twelve men, one's peers or equals. From the tithing there was an appeal to the hundred, from that to the county, and, in important cases, from that to the king. In these courts the weight of evidence was determined not so much by the character of the testimony as by the number of witnesses, and when this would not decide the cause they had recourse to the ordeal. The ordeal was of two kinds: boiling water for the common people, and red-hot iron for the nobility. If the accused took up a stone sunk to a certain depth in the boiling water, or carried the red-hot iron a certain distance without burning his hand, he was pronounced innocent; if otherwise, guilty. Sometimes cold water was used, and then if the accused sunk, he was innocent; if he swam, guilty. Another peculiar feature of their criminal jurisprudence was that all punishments were by fines, one third of which went to the judge, and the rest to the king.

It was thought highly conducive to the ends of justice to give a part of the fine to the judge, that he might be the more vigilant in ferreting out crime. Every thing, from the king's head to the tooth of a slave, had its price. By the Anglian law the value of the king's head was £1,300, that of a prince £650; a bishop's or an alderman's £350, a sheriff's £175, a clergyman's £87, and a ceorle's £21. A wound of an inch long under the hair one shilling, on the face two shillings; and whenever the criminal refused or was unable to pay his fine, he was given over to the injured party or his relatives, to be punished as they thought best. Church and State were united, both while the nation was pagan and when it became Christian. And the same body, the witenagemote, raised revenue for both, and down to the year 960 settled all disputes among the clergy. Theft and robbery were so common, until restrained by the laws of Alfred the Great, that all transfers of property above the value of twenty pence were invalid unless executed in open market and before witnesses.

Convinced that intelligence in the rulers was essential to liberty and happiness, every one who possessed two hundred acres of land or more was required to send his children to school; and inability to read and write incapacitated a man for important office. Their language was noted for its simplicity, strength, and expressiveness. The primitive words were chiefly monosyllabic, and the others were formed by uniting two or more of these, giving to each syllable a meaning. This feature shows itself especially in their proper names, of which, till the eighth century, each individual had but one, and that often indicative of his character or disposition. Some of them translated would read lion-man, tiger-man, lamb-man, noble-man, war-man, blacksmith, woodman, acre-man, etc., etc. Surnames were very rare till after the Norman conquest, but William introduced them to build up and perpetuate an aristocracy. He also changed the law of inheritance so as to make the real estate descend to the oldest son, while, by the Saxon law, the land was divided equally among all the male heirs of the deceased.

The present English language, composed as it is of words from at least twenty-six different languages, is yet five eighths Anglo-Saxon, and in these five eighths are found nearly all the terms of common life. We scold, swear, pray, and utter our proverbs in Saxon. Proverbs are to a tongue what the knots are to a pine-tree, they contain its marrow and essence; and when all else is rotted away, and gone back, as it were, to dust, the very fatness and essential oil of the language live in its proverbs. The great expressiveness and force of their language was caused by its abounding in specific terms, most of which we still retain, while our generic terms are from the Latin and Greek. To inflict a castigation is Latin; while to beat, baste, bite, bruise, box, brain, cuff, fist, cane, cleave, clip, cut, carve, cudgel; to prick, pound, nail, nip, goad, hide, maul, lick, strap, drub, knock; to foot, kick, gripe, grind, poke, nudge, elbow, ding, dint, rap, strike, whip; to wound, thrust, stick, thwack, thrash, smite, smash, squeeze, swinge, swingle, and switch, about fifty in all, each giving the kind of blow laid on, are Anglo-Saxon. It is the Saxon element which gives such beauty and power to the style of the English Bible, and of Shakspeare, Milton, Byron, and in our own country, Webster. That vigor and utility of thought which characterizes the Saxon race requires this style for its expression. It is terse, concise, clear, and strong. Every American scholar should cultivate it. In this age of steam, electricity, and science, we have not time for the ponderous sentences and choice Latinity of the style of Dr. Johnson.

The prevailing vice of the Saxons, one which ran through every rank of society from the king to the meanest slave, and one which their descendants in too great a degree inherit, was beastly drunkenness. The ale-house was among them almost a sacred place, and quarrels arising there were more severely punished than elsewhere. The lust for strong drink might justly be called the national curse of the Saxons. The dram-shop or corner groggery is, I believe, still an institution in every Anglo-Saxon country. When they conquered the Medes, in the sixth century B. C., Astyages, the king, gave them a great feast, made the leaders all drunk, slew them, and then fell upon their army and drove it out of his kingdom. Drunkenness was the greatest obstacle to their development, physical, intellectual, and moral, and may even be enumerated as one of the chief causes of their defeat by William of Normandy, for they spent the night before the battle of Hastings in riot and excess, while the more prudent Normans devoted it to sleep and prayer.

From this sketch of the political and social condition of the Anglo-Saxons at the time of the Norman Conquest, let us pass to the changes introduced by the Normans. Surnames and the law of primogeniture have already been spoken of. But the most important innovation was the feudal system. This system had already spread over the continent, but its influence was hardly felt across the British Channel till William the Conqueror divided the island among the officers of his army, and made them feudal lords. Under this system all land was supposed to belong to the king as superior lord. The barons held of him, the knights of the barons, the esquires of the knights, and the farmers of them. These last paid their rent in the products of the soil; the others, in personal services, as military attendants. The greatest deference was paid to superiors; and woman, who before, by Saxon husbands and parents, had been bought and sold, was now treated with the highest respect, nay, I might say, almost worshiped; for the Christian knight bowed the knee to his "faire ladye," and would suffer as much to vindicate her alleged ineffable beauty against all doubting knights, as he would to redeem the "Holy Sepulchre" from the hands of the infidel.

Ruled by these sentiments, the social condition of Britain rapidly improved. Law, before a rude tradition, now became a science, to excel in which required much learning; hence, for several centuries, the clergy were the lawyers. Another change was the introduction of the Norman language, and the attempt to make it supplant the Saxon. It soon prevailed at court. and among the higher classes, and would have uprooted the Saxon had not the native strength and expressiveness of the latter been too powerful for the polished periods of the former. After a long struggle the two coalesced, forming our present incomparable English; a language equal to the German for poetry and metaphysics, not excelled by the French for precision, and superior to both in copiousness and variety.

After the Norman Conquest, the next great event in Anglo-Saxon history is the English revolution. The wars with France, and the bloody civil contest between the houses of York and Lancaster, had broken the strength of the nobility; and, at the close of the sixteenth century, they were no longer able, as in the days of King John, to compel the crown to respect the rights of the people. The lords, unlike the sturdy Barons of Runnymede, who in 1215 extorted from the king the Magna Charta, saw in silence and submission royalty declare itself absolute. At this period there was a general tendency of power throughout Europe to centralization. The republics of Italy, Florence, and Genoa had fallen; the democratic spirit was crushed. The sentiment of personal independence, and personal liberty, which characterized the Gothic tribes, especially the Saxons, and which has contributed so much to the efficiency of moderate civilization, was not then strong enough to oppose the strides of despotism.

From the effect of the Crusades and the consequent reorganization of society, the old feudal and municipal liberties were lost, and new governments had arisen, more regular, centralized, and despotic. But no period exhibited a greater physical and mental activity than the fifteenth and sixteenth centuries. The Cape of Good Hope was doubled, America discovered, gunpowder and printing invented. Painting in oil had filled Europe with masterpieces of art, and engraving had multiplied and diffused them. The literary and scientific world was illumined by such lights as Cervantes, Shakspeare, and Milton, Kepler, Descartes, and Bacon. The Reformation had achieved the freedom of human reason, so that at the same time that political and civil liberty was crushed in Europe, the right of free inquiry and general emancipation of mind prevailed also and brought on a healthful reaction.

The Anglo-Saxon race naturally and logically, from the elements that composed it, was the first to assert the rights of man. A struggle began in England between the people and mind on the one hand, and the king, nobility, and wealth on the other. The result of the contest, as might be expected with a people possessing the courage, energy, and perseverance of our Saxon ancestors, was in favor of liberty.

But the Anglo-Saxon race would by no means have been able to act its rightful part in the grand drama of the world, if confined to the narrow limits of England, or restrained by kingly rule and the law of primogeniture which concentrated wealth in the hands of the few. A wider field, a freer government, a more equal distribution of property, were essential to the development of their energies and the growth and ripening of the fruits of that sentiment of personal independence, of individual liberty, which to them was coeval with their existence as a nation, or even as a tribe. The settlement of America, and her separation from the mother country at our Revolution, gave them these. The one opened a new world for their enterprise, and made every man the architect of his own fortune; the other relieved them from an hereditary aristocracy, a State Church, and the burdens which monarchy and manners and customs, the relics of a decayed system of civilization, the feudal, entailed upon them. Their history for the past century is our history and that of our mother country. It is familiar to us all. The Declaration of Independence, the War of the Revolution, Washington and the cluster of great names that make the most brilliant constellation in our political firmament; the Articles of Confederation, the Federal Constitution, that most perfect political document that ever emanated from the mind of man, and under which we have prospered beyond reasonable desire; the War of 1812, the Mexican War, and the wonderful expansion of the British empire through her colonies and conquests till it compasses the globe, are all known to the boy of the free common school. I need not recount them. And last, but not least, the great war for the rights of man which our generation, by the blessing of God, has had the singular good fortune to wage, has removed from our country, from all countries where our speech is the mother tongue, the last great relic of barbarism, and the last great bar to Anglo-Saxon progress, human slavery, and permits the American Anglo-Saxon race to follow without hinderance its instincts of freedom and human rights, and to achieve its high destiny.

"The Eastern nations sink, their glory ends,
And empire rises where the sun descends."

There is an old Anglo-Saxon proverb, "Blood will tell." It tells constantly in their history, and will continue to tell till the race has done its work. The strength of this strain of blood is manifest in the fact that it crosses with all cognate races, and takes up and absorbs their good qualities without losing its own identity, or failing to manifest and obey its own characteristics. It survived the contact with the Medes and Persians without becoming enervated. It sustained itself in a thousand years' journey with other Goths across the continent of Europe to the mouth of the Elbe, uncrushed. It mingled with the Romans and Franks, and the older Celts of Britain, without loss. It swallowed up and incorporated into itself the vikings and Danes, but threw off their freebootery. It came out all the purer and better from passing under the Normans. In America it unites with the Celt, the German, the Swede, and the Norwegian, and still remains the same, only improved. These other races, and the languages they speak, in a few generations disappear in the Anglo-Saxon American, who is now, and bids fair to be for centuries to come, the best composite, harmonious development, the highest perfection of humanity.

The two great branches of this race have put aside war in a memorable international difficulty, and settled by arbitration, in a council chamber at Geneva, grave and annoying questions that among other races would have deluged a continent in blood. The judgment pronounced by a peaceful umpire has been performed with a promptness and precision that is an example to all other races and nations.

That arbitration and its results are an epoch in the history of man. It calls to mind the prophetic lines of Virgil uttered just nineteen hundred years before:—

> "Jam redit et virgo, redeunt Saturnia regna.
> Jam nova progenies coelo dimittitur alto."

This race carries its language, its laws, its institutions with it around the world, and by dint of their good qualities makes them prevail. Australia is becoming a new Anglo-Saxon continent; New Zealand, a new Britain. Africa is being encircled as with a string of pearls by Anglo-Saxon colonies. A few thousand countrymen of the Christian and Saxon soldier, Havelock, rule one hundred and fifty millions of East Indians; and to them China and Japan have opened their doors. Two hundred and fifty years ago they numbered but three millions, a hundred and fifty years ago seventeen millions, fifty years ago thirty-four millions, to-day ninety millions: in America forty millions, in England thirty millions, and in the rest of the world twenty millions.

This race does not possess the polish and vivacity of the French, but, with a rougher exterior, it has more real nobleness of heart, weight and fixedness of purpose. Inferior in ability to analyze, to split hairs between west and north-west sides, to determine with mathematical precision the difference between nothing and its next-door neighbor, it far excels in power of generalization, in ability to seize upon the strong points, the great landmarks of truth, and to look at things with a *practical* eye. Without the sprightliness of the Italian, or the cold taciturnity of the German, the Anglo-Saxon occupies the golden mean, his risible not sufficiently excitable to endanger his buttons, nor yet so inflexible as to delay his laugh, like the Hollander, till the day after the joke. Energetic, shrewd, calculating, he will hew out a home and make a fortune where another race would dwindle away or get a bare livelihood. In ingenuity and powers of invention he would seem by some crossing of the blood to have inherited the skill of Archimedes, who burned the enemy's ships about Syracuse with his sun-glasses, and that of Dædalus, the personification of Grecian art and mechanics, who escaped from the Cretan tyrant on wings of his own construction. He does not, like his Teutonic cousin, spend years meditating upon some abstruse principle of metaphysics—he is too much of a utilitarian for such fruitless investigations—but he gives his thoughts to the more immediate well-being of society. He sees a world full of things to do and but a short time to do them. From the school-room he plunges directly into business or politics. Of too active a temperament to be burdened with flesh, he is nervously thinking how he may make his own fortune excel that of his neighbor, or his nation surpass all others in wealth and power; or, perhaps, like his ancestors of the sixth century, he may be devising a scheme to relieve an adjacent country of a rich slice of territory and annex it to his own, without absolutely violating the law of nations. An ardent lover of the rights of man, he is a turbulent subject, but a good citizen. In war he has not the wild enthusiasm which inspired the soldiers of Napoleon, but he goes into the contest with a fixed will to win. He may not storm a redoubt, but he can fight a three days' battle.

Physically, the Anglo-Saxons are hardy, muscular, active, and energetic; mentally, clear, cool, shrewd, enterprising, and ambitious. From the necessities of their very nature they are friends of political and religious liberty, and enemies of tyrants, whether spiritual or temporal. Their mission demands for its fulfillment free government, free and universal education, a free Church, and one that recognizes man as a being gifted with reason and a free will. If the race be true to itself, if it fulfills the high destiny which the Divine hand seems to have marked out for it, then, when its cycle shall have been completed and its record made up, future races will look back upon its period as the brightest in human history.

www.ingramcontent.com/pod-product-compliance
Lightning Source LLC
LaVergne TN
LVHW011136110826
845150LV00008B/2376